# **Chakras**

A Comprehensive Guide To Activating Chakra Energy In A Sequential Manner Chakra Balancing Through The Use Of A Chakra Meditation Script: A Guide On How To Properly Align Your Chakras

*(The Comprehensive Guide To Chakra Meditation For Healing)*

**Drago Barth**

# **TABLE OF CONTNET**

Meditation's Character ............................................................. 1

The Third Eye Has A Malevolent Aspect. .................... 16

Expand On Your Work With Further Subtle Energy-Healing Methods................................................................... 38

What Does An Awakened And Balanced Throat Chakra Feel Like? .................................................................. 58

An Extremely Optimistic View Of Life: ....................... 84

Which Is The Reason For Energy (Chakra) Imbalance? ........................................................................... 112

Deep Diving Heart Chakra Reflections ..................... 135

# Meditation's Character

In my opinion, this is perhaps the most crucial lesson to learn from this book, which synthesizes a wide range of ideas and perspectives from modern and ancient meditation traditions. Thus, to sum up, I have experienced that as a meditation practitioner and instructor.

It won't look the same to everyone. Another thing you may have heard others say is that the "success" of meditation is ceasing to think when in meditation.

Is it possible to put thoughts aside? Sure, maybe for a little while. However, not if we wish to carry on leading kind and social lives as humans. Not really. Not permanently. We all possess what the ancient yogis called manas, or a "thinking machine," that is fundamental to who we are and what it is like to live in this world.

Most people have experienced "flow experiences" at some point in their lives, where thinking, feeling, and acting merge into one via a complete focus on the present moment, and thoughts almost vanish. But our main objective in meditation is not to become thoughtless or to allow our thoughts to stop flowing. While it is a lovely sensation when this occurs occasionally, in my opinion, as a meditation practitioner and instructor, it is more of an amusement value than a true accomplishment.

The experience of meditation itself is not the ultimate measure of a meditation practice's worth; rather, it is determined by how it impacts your daily life!

This seemingly insignificant realization is sometimes difficult to grasp, particularly when we actually get quite powerful sensations or happy states during our meditation that we would like to stay in.

Our ego says, "I want more of this; this is how it should always be," far too rapidly. Then, usually, we become consumed with trying to replicate a state that is impossible to replicate in the same way. It is difficult to avoid, particularly after a highly intense experience.

But if we only remember this, it already helps. In other words, I'll reiterate it based on its significance:

If we truly want to advance as human beings, if we desire an embodied awakening rather than merely a separated ego journey to Master Heaven, then we need to incorporate meditation into our daily lives.

Practicing formal meditation helps us become more and more present and mindful in our daily lives. Thus, meditation is a powerful tool for identifying and weakening, or even better, transforming, unhelpful thought and behavior patterns. It is an amplifier for almost any attempt to know ourselves better. Samskara is the term used in yoga to describe these patterns and impressions.

The term "tantric approach" refers to the application of spirituality to everything that exists in our lives without categorizing things as "spiritual" or "non-spiritual." Examples of this approach include Hatha yoga, the Kashmiri tantra paths, Osho's teachings, and Daoist inner qigong.

I shall be referring to this theory frequently in this book and would like to speak a few things about it now because I have just introduced the term tantra. I use the phrases yoga, Tantra, and meditation interchangeably in my workshops.

This interpretation of Tantra has little to do with the so-called neo-tantra, which emphasizes sexual and social experience, either as a means (spiritual liberation through the release of sexual energies) or as an end in itself (sexual liberation and increase of ecstatic potential, resolution of old traumas and strengthening of a more loving, mindful interaction).

As a practitioner, I see myself as associated with this path's traditional form based on the ideas of inner freedom and the interconnectedness of all things.

Tantra translates to "net" or "web," implying that everything in the universe is intricately linked. For example, all Hatha yoga styles have their roots in Tantra and originally united mind and body without devaluing the physical body.

That's everything for Tantra for now. Later on, we shall delve into further detail, particularly in Chapter 4, which is devoted entirely to this idea.

This book is about the principles that underpin all meditative experiences. While it is influenced by tantric meditation (based on my experience as a practitioner), it is also about meditation in general. It may interest both novices and experienced practitioners of all orientations.

Meditation is a tool to help us be more present and intense in our daily lives, increase our awareness, and progress ever closer to inner freedom and authenticity.

Once we practice meditation to a certain degree, we may experience a feeling that our actions "just happen"—that is, that, although still based on our conscious choices, they seem ingrained in a higher purpose that our little egos can never fully know—nor need to know. In other words, our actions seem so spontaneous and in the best interest of all involved.

The majority of societies have long been aware of the third sight. Despite the lack of communication tools at the time, their portrayals and worldviews are comparable. This indicates that some of these cultures were aware of the third eye.

People who have discovered the third eye's secret have kept it a secret across civilizations because they either wanted all of the potential for themselves or didn't want this power to fall into the wrong hands. The third eye opens the practitioner's mind. You would stop being a follower and become a leader as your wisdom grows. This could be one of the reasons the third eye's abilities were kept a secret.

Those in positions of authority want others to follow them. This is only possible if those who live in lower social strata find it difficult to exist. The mechanics of power drive our world. Those at the top frequently attempt to exercise personal control over authority. This is a major factor in limiting instruction to tutoring sessions. The Holy Bible was composed in an incomprehensible language to the general public. The masses were only fed topics that contributed to their domination.

The third eye has proven to be the same. Prominent figures worldwide were aware of and have utilized the third eye's abilities. However, the general public was unaware of the third eye's mysteries. Only the rumor that seeped down from the top was known to the public. It is portrayed as having the ability to do significant damage. It's also claimed that not everyone can control or activate the muscles of the third eye.

The majority of these beliefs are unfounded. We will now talk about five third-eye myths and their integrity.

1. Since the Third Eye is closed in most of us, not everyone can use it. It's only open to a select few.

One of the biggest lies you may fall into is this one. Everybody possesses the third eye. This metaphysical eye is physically located in the pineal gland. Everybody has it. It is a gland that serves your body's multiple essential purposes. You would be in a terrible situation if you didn't have the pineal gland. You would experience irregular sleep and wakefulness patterns and no sensation of enjoyment. The pineal gland tells you about day and night and controls your body's circadian rhythms. We do not have a completely closed third eye. The fact that we are all capable of intuition proves that, if imperfectly, the third eye is active in every one of us. Thus, the myth's initial portion is unfounded. Everybody has the physical gland required for the third eye to function properly. The third eye can be fully awakened and utilized. It is unnecessary to be a specific person or incarnation to open the third eye in a person or image. Anyone willing to dedicate time to meditation can open the third eye.

Dedication is all that is needed to open the third eye. You'll need to hone your abilities and choose the meditation route. We all have the pineal gland but must cultivate our higher awareness, intuition, and foresight. You will be able to experience these powers more fully if you meditate. This can be done regardless of your color, class, or religion. The third eye is a spiritual rather than religious idea.

2. You should try opening your third eye.

Within you is the third eye. You might be able to open your third eye without the assistance of others. The powers of the third eye will become indispensable to you if you decide to use them and begin working on the proper path. On your path, you can get assistance from teachers, enlightened beings, and persons with developed psychic talents. But you would be gravely incorrect if you thought that was a power someone could bestow upon you. You are being misled if someone has been telling you this.

To open your third eye, you need commitment and effort, but you do not need others. Learn how to open your third eye and proceed along the path if you wish to do so.

3. Some folks have instantaneous third eye-opening.

It is not necessary to implant the third eye inside of you. You already have this physical gland within you. For most of us, the psychic aspect of the third eye is dormant since we hardly utilize it. However, that does not mean someone flipping a switch might open your third eye. You must develop your consciousness since it is yours. If you provide it the attention it deserves, you can simply extend your third eye.

It could take some time, and you might not notice anything remarkable at first. Your third eye must first be awakened before you may strengthen its abilities. It's like working out with an iron. You grow better at it the more you practice. Although they can't generate muscle for you, a skilled instructor or coach can help you develop your physique more quickly. While some people can open their third eye on the first session, others do not. That being said, anyone can open their third eye.

## The Third Eye Has A Malevolent Aspect.

By definition, no power is good or bad. The character of energy is determined by how it is used. The third eye is in the same boat. Several psychic powers can be developed with the use of the third eye. People can benefit from certain psychic skills if they are applied appropriately. They might, however, be employed for evil purposes or to harm others. There will be repercussions for the person who started it as well.

Negative energies build up if someone uses their third-eye abilities for evil. It will significantly alter the way you think and who you are. You wouldn't stay the same individual. It's crucial to use these powers wisely.

5. Knowing that your third eye is engaged would be beneficial.

Nothing could be further from the reality. The internet spreads false information, suggesting that when your third eye emerges, you will have certain experiences. It's similar to controlling the uncontrollable. The third eye opens the portal to a different dimension. There are countless options. Your experiences could differ greatly from one another. You are euphoric even though you may not experience what other people have described.

Everybody will experience third-eye differently. The mental process begins as soon as your third eye opens. Your behavior will begin to shift. Opening your third eye won't give you rapid access to psychic abilities. It is possible that you won't experience any changes even after your third eye awakens. You won't notice a difference in your awareness and perception until after consistent practice.

Words of Wisdom for the Throat Chakra

Remember that the vagus nerve goes through the throat and vocal cords; thus, singing and humming can activate this nerve. This is why the seed mantra ham, pronounced hum, can have amazing effects. The freedom to express who you truly are will be the main theme of the English affirmations.

● I listen to my inner voice ● I speak the truth ● I communicate authentically ● My voice matters and is heard ● My words help others ● I actively confront my emotions ● I express my emotions fearlessly ● I have integrity ● I have the guts to defend myself

Recall that for affirmations to be effective, you must believe them. For this reason, it's crucial to address each chakra in turn. If your heart chakra is out of balance and you are not emotionally aware, it is not beneficial to work on emotional communication. Now that we have this in mind, we may discuss the third eye chakra.

Chapter 8: Ajna's Third Eye Chakra

The third eye chakra is higher on the brow than in the space between your eyes. "Beyond wisdom, perception, or command" is what ajna means. Feminine energy and spirituality are profoundly connected. It is connected to the light element. The pineal gland, which links light, day, and night, is linked to the chakra. The pineal gland produces the hormones serotonin and melatonin, essential to our sleep cycles.

The throat is the first entry point into consciousness, whereas the third eye chakra is traditionally considered the "eye of consciousness." Consider this chakra the hub of your self-awareness, intuition, and wisdom. The final chakra on the physical body, the third eye chakra, is responsible for our creativity and imagination. It gives us a visionary viewpoint and aids in concretizing our reality based on what we choose to see in the outside world. More faith in our inner voice is possible when we let go of binary thinking and heed our inner guidance.

The two-petalled lotus is blue with a triangle facing downward in the center. The petals are the powers of the sun and moon, respectively, known as pringala and ida. Starting from the root chakra, these energy lines ascend to the nostrils. The inner triangle stands for enlightenment.

How to Recognize an Unbalanced Third Eye Chakra

On a physical level, tension headaches are possible, particularly in the brow area. Health problems can affect your vision, or your eyesight might not be at its optimum. You might get migraines, vertigo, nasal issues, or neurological conditions.

A weak third eye chakra might cause one to lack creativity and have trouble establishing plans or setting objectives. It frequently comes with a stuck perspective, which holds that you are limited in what you can learn and become better at. You may be hiding some parts of your existence. If your chakra is blocked, you may feel like you are in a rut and cannot discern your life's purpose. You can sense that something is off, but you're unsure. You can be oppressed by a cloud of pessimism and reject your spirituality instead of embracing it. An overactive chakra might make it difficult for you to focus and cause hallucinations, paranoia, or nightmares.

When the third eye chakra is balanced, you will have excellent memory and recall, including the ability to recall your dreams. Your alertness, optimism, and intuition will all be stronger. Overall, you'll feel happy and excited, and you'll feel more in control.

How to Harmonize the Third Eye Chakra

In addition to yoga, third-eye chakra unblocking can be achieved via meditation. Since not everyone can meditate for extended periods, we will start with the steps and don't feel the need to start with that. To begin with, try a short few minutes.

Meditating

Locate a peaceful, comfortable area where you won't be bothered. If sitting on a cushion, chair, or meditation seat is more comfortable, you can lie down.

As you get more accustomed to the practice, progressively extend the timer from the initial few minutes.

If it feels comfortable, close your eyes and inhale deeply several times. Let your mind and body unwind.

Pay close attention to your breathing and the sensation of air entering and leaving your body. If counting your breath aids in maintaining attention, then do so.

When your thoughts stray (as they will), gently return them to your breathing without passing judgment on yourself. Watch the thoughts come and go, trying not to get attached to them.

If you are having trouble focusing on your breathing, you may find that a mantra, visualization, or meditation helps you stay in the present.

After the timer goes off, carefully open your eyes and take a few deep breaths. Just be aware of your feelings for a time without passing judgment or dissecting the situation.

Either lie on the floor or gently sit on a chair to ensure comfort. Feet on the ground, hands resting in your lap.

After taking note of your physical experiences, take a moment to rest while keeping an eye on the ambient noise and room temperature.

Bring in the orange hue of the twilight now. Let your orange light envelop you in your Hara, which is the source of drive, balance, and empowerment. Feed your Hara and recite the incantations, "I at this moment will allow my spirit to be fully nourished," and "I will honor all of my sacred personal needs."

When ready, focus on the gentle area directly beneath your breastbone. This is the chakra of personal power, where your solar plexus is located.

Now start inhaling, letting your solar plexus soften and gradually expanding your breathing. Now experience the warmth and comfort of an orange light casting a shadow over you, and feel the strength and confidence within yourself.

Inhale the revitalizing energy that this self-confidence brings. Inhale deeply into your sacral chakra, which originates your inner strength. Experience this feeling of strength, motivation, and empowerment. Observe your ideas without passing judgment. Do they have greater authority? Do you think you're psychologically stronger now? Let yourself be aware of these thoughts without passing judgment on them or trying to alter them in any way.

Breathe in and out while repeating the movement in your abdomen with rhythm and harmony. As you inhale and exhale, feel your body expanding.

Accept all pleasant sensations and ideas without judging them—just express gratitude for them. While you maintain the rhythm of your breathing, let them enliven you.

Now let the orange glow envelop and cover you. This light is warm to the touch.

Breathe in and out in time with the soothing color, and while you do so, notice how the sacral chakra gives you personal strength. Rest in this awareness.

With your hands in your lap and your feet on the ground, experience the actual feelings of your body right now. When you're prepared, rise and open your eyes.

Take a big breath on Day 6. As you release your breath, focus on the area directly below your navel on your abdomen. Imagine now having an orange chakra that is bright and glowing inside you. This radiant orange chakra starts to ripple throughout your body like little waves on a silky lake surface. You feel like the smooth, flowing waves gently washing up on the body's shore.

Now imagine yourself sitting calmly, shortly before sunrise, on a beach with white sand. The orange hue of the sky is now vividly striped, waiting for the sun to rise. Gaze upward at the heavens.

Lift your eyes to the wide, peaceful expanse of water before you. Step forward and gently dip your toe into the ocean's warmth. Observe how it approaches you gradually, lap around both of your feet and then move back into the ocean.

The waves now start to hug your thighs and knees as you advance. You can see the white sand floor beneath your feet and the crystal clear water below. You dive into the water and begin to swim with ease. Now, you simply turn onto your back and start floating like a leaf without weight.

You have been moving slowly and softly, flowing with the waves while staring at the vivid orange sky.

Your second chakra is currently spiraling and becoming more powerful. It begins to rotate more quickly. Your body is bathed in orange light, permeating every pore and cell.

Calm down within this consciousness. Resuming your swimming slowly will help you feel secure and surrounded by tranquility.

When you're all set, get up and open your eyes.

Modify your nutrition

You could not be waking up at all because of your nutrition. What kind of energy do the foods you eat contain? Have you ever thought about looking for something? You've probably thought about the food's protein, fat, carbohydrate, and calorie composition, but have you thought about how it vibrates? Eating food rich in vibrational power is necessary to awaken the source of subtle yet universal energy inside you. If you're experiencing problems with awakening that don't seem related to anything else, you might consider changing your diet. Replace processed foods with whole ones. Replace meat with fresh produce. Your cells can refill their nutrient stores more readily if you eat and drink a nutrient-rich diet. This will make you appear better and feel better on the outside! It may sound strange, but food, like crystals and herbs, has energy. You are the product of what you eat; thus, if most of you eat is dead, you will continue to have low vibration. Elevate your energy through your diet, and the earth-shattering waves of enlightenment, known as Shakti, will carry your Kundalini.

Spend time outdoors and practice meditation.

Don't overlook the importance of getting some exercise and fresh air as you begin this life-changing practice. You might go through periods of low energy when you let go of things that aren't helping you. There will be moments when you think your vitality is going to burst. You'll have times when it seems like you've been walking around with blinders and are only now beginning to see the forest for the trees.

During this strange and perplexing moment of Kundalini rising, having a solid grounding habit can be quite helpful. Remember how important it is to spend time outside as you proceed. Nature has an almost infinite supply of delicate bodily healing powers. It's brimming with hints that will enable you to establish communication with your spirit guides, intuition, and higher self. The ground we walk on is alive, and although its lessons are so eternally important, they can teach us more about ourselves and our potential as human beings than we would choose to hear or learn. Whenever possible, go outside, wherever you may be in the world. Put on attire appropriate for the weather and go outside to appreciate nature! These beautiful settings have visual symbolism that will support your kundalini energy as you tackle the difficult work.

Consider volunteering or leading a life of service.

Do your actions stem from a pure heart? If not, do you follow your instincts or reason while making decisions? Maybe you're just winging it out of your crotch. Many self-discoveries will be necessary to raise the Kundalini and clear the chakras. As you have insight into how your self-expression has been (or has not been) compatible with your overall growth, you'll start to notice recurring patterns and peculiarities in your personality. You may have to acknowledge your limitations in relationships, self-control, creativity, resilience, spirituality, telepathy, and other areas where you have room to grow.

But the hardest flaw to face (especially for those worried about Kundalini rising) is the inability to love unconditionally and fully. "Faking it until you make it" won't likely assist people with problems because their heart chakra is blocked. You need something material or someone to relate to for this love to feel genuine to you. In such a case, you could try volunteering or taking a temporary job change to engage in some sort of service activity. Your ability to love people selflessly will be tested and strengthened when you put yourself in a position of service at work. Though it's not a given, your impressions might be completely favorable. But have faith—your most difficult experiences will teach you the most. Your heart opens out and blossoms with every new experience, just like a flower does. When you find yourself responding to the things that used to aggravate you the most with love, the Kundalini has awakened.

**Expand On Your Work With Further Subtle Energy-Healing Methods.**

Other subtle energy-healing techniques can support a kundalini awakening in addition to using healing stones and spending time in nature. Furthermore, as you learn more about subtle energy-healing techniques, you'll instinctively begin to blend and blend techniques as you see fit. You will discover that your intuition, or connection to your higher self and beyond, is more powerful and beneficial than almost anything else as you discover what works and what doesn't. You will draw the healing you require as a plant, massage, or a small pill that dissolves under your tongue. As such, you should always incorporate other subtle energetic modalities into your kundalini awakening practice (or any other kind of awakening or ascension, for that matter) as you see fit. The following is a list of several options.

To help with your kundalini awakening, you could start by experimenting with floral essences as a mild energy healing therapy. Flower essences are made by extracting and utilizing a particular flower's vibration. Put a few flower buds (or the product made from them) in a glass dish filled with water. After that, the bowl is exposed to direct sunshine for a full day. You can complete this in one go or over several days. After removing the flower buds, a small amount of brandy is added to the water before bottling it as a preservative. The essences of flowers are those! The exciting part is about to begin. Like every person, color, and crystal, every flower has its frequency. The medicine can be taken orally (a few drops of its liquid taken multiple times a day) to address issues related to one's aura or subtle energetic expression once the flower's "essence" has been "extracted," to some extent, in the floral essence. Additionally, flower essences can unblock chakras without you realizing it. The possibilities with floral essences will astound you, so I strongly advise you to learn more about them.

Secondly, to clear your chakras and hasten the kundalini process, you can consider having reiki therapy. Reiki healing is a traditional Japanese energy work practice where the practitioner channels her wisdom and strength into the circumstance to release the recipient from internal barriers or difficulties. While massage is frequently combined with reiki therapy, it is not required. The primary goal of Reiki is for the practitioner to remove energy blockages from the recipient without coming into contact with them. The techniques used by reiki practitioners can work even when they are not there. Guidance to break open your chakras from other states and allow the serpent energy to flow freely within you is available to those who have successfully connected their Kundalini to Shakti, their spirit guides, and the earth. It's critical to go into your first session with reasonable expectations.

Third, getting a massage can help release obstructions and is widely accessible. In any case, massages—with or without Reiki—are wonderful. They have additional advantages besides feeling fantastic for your skin and muscles (especially when done by a trustworthy person). Any blockages you may be experiencing as you progress through the chakra opening and clearing process (i.e., through where it feels okay to be touched and where it doesn't, through the places the masseuse tends to linger on, through pains you didn't know you had, and more). A manicure or pedicure (even for a man!) or a massage is too much for you. Step up, schedule the meeting, and assume leadership! The manicurist or pedicurist will certainly massage your hands or feet. Because reflexology works locally, this massage will profoundly impact your body-wide awareness (and potentially even trigger a kundalini awakening). Any kind of reflexology, acupuncture, or acupressure may have the same effects on you.

Finally, counseling is always an option if you feel ready to pursue it. Sometimes, even though it's not always effective, simply talking things out can have a profound impact. In therapy, talking is not the sole approach. As you may remember earlier in this chapter, the healing process can benefit greatly from music, color, sound, and art. If you need assistance handling a problem that is bigger than you can handle alone, don't feel guilty about asking for it. It might save your life to give counseling a try. It can be challenging to decide the right first action to take. If you have access to it, start with art therapy or music. If you don't have the money for private medical care, you can try doing treatments yourself. By all means, speak with a "shrink" or counselor if that's what's necessary to neutralize and remove the toxicity. Kundalini and your higher self will be grateful for your efforts.

The sixth alternative is using essential oils or natural medicines to get things started. These suggestions are linked by their reliance on the phantom energies of different plants and herbs. Herbs can extract vibration and preserved as essential oils or "flower" essences. However, their subtle therapeutic properties make them valuable when using herbs for healing. While it can be difficult to find essential oils, herbs are frequently simple to gather from your yard.

Today, you can purchase online even if you're pressed for time. Invest in essential oils that align perfectly with your goals, and intentionally keep things low-tech and ceremonial. Taking a field guide with you will help you identify plants in the wild if you would rather forego technology and chance your luck. Find out what kind of plant it is, and if something draws your attention, record it down. You may have the best course of treatment all along by listening to your guides' guidance. Other you use a store-bought plant, an essential oil, or an herb you have wild-harvested, Kundalini will react favorably.6. Another alternative is to decalcify your pineal gland and reprogram your energy by staring at the sun. You'll need to spend every morning and evening outside to engage in real sun gazing. The main idea is to face the sun at dawn and sunset, stand barefoot in the sunlight, and allow the sun's healing energy to enter you. This approach can help you experience a deeper sense of oneness with the land when combined with intermittent or spontaneous fasting. Sungazing is said to provide health benefits that are difficult to equal with traditional medical care, such as a decrease in the signs and symptoms of sickness, aging, and hunger. To benefit from the sun's healing rays, rise before it does. If, after a week, you didn't feel the Kundalini bringing forth some shakti within you, I would be shocked.

Finally, you may try homeopathic remedies if you have trouble cleansing your chakras. We investigate the more traditional practice of homeopathy (like cures like) about subtle energy remedies, as opposed to the allopathic healing philosophies underlying drugs and mainstream medicine. Homeopathy is well worth your time and attention, even with its bad reputation. To treat symptoms, homeopathic medications mimic the energy fingerprints of many things, including minerals, plants, and animals. In contrast to traditional medicine, which maintains that every sickness needs a different course of therapy, homeopathy maintains that poisons—in very small amounts—can treat more serious conditions. Look into homeopathy if this subject interests you; it is worthy of a book. A small homeopathic tablet that you dissolve under your tongue may trigger your kundalini awakening. The nicest thing about using homeopathic medicines is that they won't harm you in any way if you take ones that your body doesn't need. These lovely, sensitive, dynamic treatments work only if you need them. Why do you hesitate so much? You won't know how beneficial these therapies can be until you complete the required reading and try them.

Chapter 7: Chakra Correspondences for Healing the Throat

What Functions the Throat Chakra and What Makes It Significant?

The throat chakra, the fifth chakra in your body, impacts your communication ability. It also gives you the confidence to advocate for yourself. It is sometimes referred to as the truth or vanguard chakra since it can assist you in expressing your truth. The throat chakra is a great place to learn about integrity and honesty, two crucial life skills.

Many people don't employ these qualities since they are denigrated by those who don't lead morally upright lives. The central region of the neck is home to the throat chakra. It is a crucial component because it pertains to your connections with other people. This chakra must be open and balanced in your life to express your thoughts, sentiments, and emotions without feeling intimidated by those around you.

The Effects of a Blocked Throat Chakra on the Body

You will feel soreness in your throat when this chakra is obstructed. You might even occasionally become voiceless. You might also experience issues with your thyroid, heartburn, indigestion, mouth ulcers, and eating disorders. Dental and hearing problems are also not unheard of. Since the ears, mouth, and throat are associated with this chakra, these body parts will suffer severe consequences if your Vishuddha imbalance or blockage remains untreated for an extended period. This does not imply that you should forego seeing a doctor to treat them; rather, it suggests that you look into doing chakra work to aid with the healing and recovery process and, more importantly, to support your ability to fully live and express your truth.

## Impact of a Blocked Throat Chakra on Emotions

You could find it difficult to express your opinions to people around you if your throat chakra is obstructed. It's also possible for you to treat other people as though they should be able to read your thoughts, even though not everyone is. You never know what they're thinking or feeling. You can be expecting too much of them and putting too much pressure on them to comprehend you.

Another issue is finding it difficult to voice your concerns when they arise. You either find yourself speaking things that don't make sense, or you find yourself bottling things up. Because of this persistent knot of worry in your stomach and threats that are mostly unfounded—at least not for you and your experiences—you may feel alone, uneasy being honest with others, and even worse with yourself. It's understandable how having a persistent sense of threat could lead to shoulder and neck pain as it keeps you on edge and conscious of what you say. You pay attention to what you say and what your body and lips are not saying. It's a horrible way to live, and if you identify with this, you need to take action to bring this chakra into balance so you can breathe easier. Living in continual rage at hiding your truth and paranoia is not worth it.

## Impact of a Blocked Throat Chakra on Spirituality

You can experience a loss of spiritual connection or hearing from the divine. Feeling like you are nothing more than your physical self is a strange feeling. Even though your spirit guides try to communicate with you, you cannot receive even a single message from them. As a result, you frequently find yourself in circumstances you could have avoided had you paid attention to their advice. It's simple to claim that you don't get messages from your spirit guides as you don't think you've ever had the gift of prophecy. However, the truth is that we all do. There are many other ways that clairaudience might appear, so it's not a guarantee that you have never experienced it.

Therefore, when your throat chakra is blocked, you effectively block your divine spirit's ability to reach out to you and speak your truth into the world. Consider the chakra in your throat as an ear. That may seem a little strange, but bear with me. You can influence the course of your world and share the essence of who you are with those around you by using your throat chakra. Stated differently, it is a vital energy hub for materialization. Your throat chakra is a receiving area for information blocks or downloads from the spirit realm that may help you manifest your life goals, so it serves many more purposes than just letting you express your ideas. Since we are all spirits at our heart, when this chakra is out of balance, you might not get clear information, and when it is blocked, you might feel as though you are cut off from what makes you, yourself.

What Throat Chakra Blocks?

Your throat chakra may close if you smoke or drink, among other filthy, unsavory activities. Purification is the meaning of the Sanskrit term for the throat chakra. Therefore, consuming unhealthy food is one way that could obstruct this chakra. Additionally, negative thoughts about other individuals may obstruct your throat chakra. Therefore, be aware of the thoughts you entertain to avoid creating obstacles. When the chips are down, there's always a temptation to lie and flatter someone because, let's face it, it's difficult to tell them the bad things you think of them. These are the kinds of things that can throw this energy center out of balance.

## What Does An Awakened And Balanced Throat Chakra Feel Like?

You are not afraid to express your emotions when your throat chakra is open. You no longer allow those things to stop you from expressing your truth, even though it's not as though you are unaware of the consequences. You realize that you cannot protect people from their feelings; therefore, even if they take offense at what you say, you will speak the truth. This does not imply that you turn into an awful person. It just means that you won't let your anxiety about other people's reactions keep you silent. If anything, bringing your throat chakra into balance will ensure that you can speak with love and all the truth.

Speaking loudly is another fascinating thing that happens to persons who have balanced their throat chakra. When I say loud, I mean confidently loud, not loud, as in annoying. Additionally, there's a melodic quality to their speech. When the throat chakra of a person who was talkative due to an overactive throat chakra is balanced in this area, the person realizes they are not talking as much as they once did. Instead of waiting to speak, they might stop and hear what the other person says. You can bring balance to this energy area by eliminating gossip and becoming unintentionally dishonest to create drama. Additionally, you cease interjecting while others are attempting to speak.

You'll discover that problems that you previously faced, such as swallowing and lockjaw, thyroid troubles, neck and ear pain, and voice loss, are now in the past. And all digestive problems will be resolved.

Chakras have existed for a significant amount of human history. They have aided humans in developing a more comprehensive awareness of their bodies and minds for millennia. We can use this approach to categorize various aspects of our lives and explain our thoughts and emotions. Chakras have played a significant role in helping those who want a deeper connection with their bodies. We will lay out some of the most important characteristics of chakras in this pillar to help you start your chakra journey. To help you better understand what chakras are and do, let us first give you a general understanding of them. After that, we'll discuss a few widespread myths regarding chakras. After that, we'll explore the practice's beginnings and development from antiquity to the present. We will finally talk about chakras and how they relate to energy. You will have a foundational knowledge of chakras by the time you finish this pillar, which will help you throughout the rest of the book.

Buddhism

Though it certainly has ancient roots, Buddhism is a relatively modern religion compared to Hinduism. Buddhism originated in what is now the northern part of the country of India circa 500 B.C.E. Siddhartha, a prince, was the one who started it all when he decided to give up his life in the aristocracy and live among the impoverished to arrive at a universal knowledge of reality. Thus, Buddhist teachings assert that selflessness is the only authentic representation of reality and that there are no genuine boundaries between humans and animals or between people and people. From nce, Buddhism expanded throughout the Asian subcontinent and into China, Korea, and Japan, where it is still practiced extensively today.

Though Buddhism and Hinduism are fundamentally distinct, many Hindu ideas have been incorporated into Buddhism since it was founded in South

Asia. While the early Buddhist writings do not explicitly discuss chakras, some common misconceptions can be traced back to Hindu chakra practice. The most common application of the chakras in Buddhism is found in Tibetan Buddhism, a specific branch of Buddhism that has heavily incorporated Hindu concepts into its theology. Chakra meditation, as in Hinduism, has a strong heritage in Tibetan Buddhism. Chakra or energy exercises are used in different Buddhist traditions, nevertheless. In Chinese or Zen Buddhism, for instance, there are three primary chakras recognized: the lower dantian, which is comparable to the solar plexus or sacral region; the middle dantian, which is comparable to the heart or neck; and the higher dantian; which is comparable to the third eye or crown. The Hindu chakra system has origins that we may see in this chakra exercise. Therefore, there are elements of chakra healing found in Buddhism, even if chakras aren't as central to Buddhist religion as they are in Hinduism.

You will experience more worry and anxiety the wider the gap is, not just in social settings but also outside of them.

You have to acknowledge that shame if you want to get past it. Shame is only the dread of not being good enough. When you show others who you are, warts and all, you become unworthy of their love and respect.

First of all, we are all incredibly flawed, as I'm sure you already know. Furthermore, we tend to overvalue other individuals when, in reality, they don't.

It is not our place to blame when others become alarmed when we reveal our imperfect but unique selves to the world. It will also be crucial to let go of this situation, go with the flow, and watch what occurs.

While I was studying and practicing how to overcome my own anxiety and panic attacks, I wanted to explain how I handled restaurant scenarios. We'll review every tactic you can use in part two and the supplement.

When I was back in a restaurant, the nausea and other symptoms reappeared exactly as they had in the good old days. They never skipped a dinner at a restaurant. Initially, I experienced the same rise in worry as before, asking myself, "Djeezs, why is this happening now? I mean, my plate is still incredibly full. I'm eating nonstop right now! If I do, the waiter will question me about what went wrong with it.

However, I changed my direction afterward.

I started to think, "Wait, stop." The waiter is irrelevant. I am who I am. It is entirely up to me whether or not I want to give up eating for ANY reason. It's up to me to make that decision. I'll handle it if I pass out and make a big deal out of it! We might make fun of me at future Christmas gatherings if I pass out, break out rashly, or look foolish in any other way. Who cares if I choose to live happily ever after, hidden under a rock? I'm following the current. If the nausea disappears, I'll wait until then and quit eating. I'm probably queasy because I ate something that my body didn't like.

Remarkably, if I had consumed one of the substances to stay away from, the nausea would frequently persist, but the worry would go away. In every other instance, when the discomfort had been solely attributed to the social restaurant environment, even the nausea subsided as soon as I was willing to let go and stop feeling guilty about it.

And it did happen that I was asked by others, "Is everything okay?I then always opted to be genuine and true to myself, saying things like, "Well, my hunger is gone all of a sudden." That seems a little strange. How is the food tasting for you?"

We must learn to accept our individuality and stop making such a huge deal out of everything.

Inherited?

Some nervous persons discover that they are not the only members of their family who experience higher levels of anxiety than usual. It appears that anxiousness may run in the family in some cases. This indicates that you may be more worried than the average person due to your genetic makeup. One of your parents likely shared your traits if you are an HSP (highly sensitive person). First off, there's good news here. My grandfather and father were extremely nervous men who loved to worry about the little things in life. My father, in particular, has a lot of anxiety tendencies. Every Sunday, he would suffer from migraine headaches just because Monday meant returning to work. I must have anxiety all the time since it runs in my family, isn't that right?

Not true. Yes, because my disposition made me more worried than the typical, non-anxious Joe, it forced me to walk down the path that led to Panic Ville. However, you can pack your bags and head back whenever you decide. I wouldn't have been able to fully overcome my panic attacks over ten years ago if they were inherited. All your genes do is predispose you. a lock. Whether you turn the key or not is still up to you.

Considering everyone I've assisted, I think learned behavior is far more important. Your nervous parents have likely influenced your world perspective if you had them as children.

For instance, did you know babies are fearless around snakes and spiders? According to studies, when children hear their mother respond negatively to the spider that one morning was cautiously slithering down the shower curtain, they develop a fear of spiders.

We tend to adopt many of our contemporaries' worries as we age. This is something that, in my opinion, can contribute to the perception of anxiety as inherited when, in reality, it's a learned behavior.

What is the one thing that some parents tell their kids repeatedly? "Take caution!"

The most noticeable sign of a blocked third eye chakra is the sensation that you cannot access the wisdom within and around you. Anger, annoyance, and uncertainty are just a few ways this lack of access might show themselves. It may also appear that these symptoms are exclusive to an obstruction in the eye chakra. Still, these symptoms may appear even after you have begun to correct your chakras. We'll go into more detail about this topic in the upcoming chapter.

The following are some emotional and mental signs of a third eye chakra in balance:

**Enhanced mental and expressive clarity:** When the third eye chakra opens, we can finally perceive things more clearly. We think clearly and communicate ourselves clearly and concisely. Considering a confusing thought is one of the finest ways to verify this. This might be an unclear circumstance for you or someone you're unsure about. It's likely that despite having access to all the information, you're finding it difficult to identify how you truly feel about the situation. You'll know exactly how you feel about the circumstance when your third eye chakra wakes. Go back and review it. Additionally, you'll be able to communicate your ideas to others clearly and concisely.

**Improved memory and concentration:** You'll concentrate better in the present if your third eye chakra is in alignment. Additionally, you'll be able to recall events and individuals for what they truly were rather than for what you wish. Because memory is such a fickle organ, it occasionally cooperates with our efforts to ignore unpleasant realities. To help you feel comfortable in the future, you might, for instance, find yourself ignoring the specifics of an unpleasant past event. We can occasionally be protected by our (lack of) memory, but anyone who genuinely wishes to change and heal will not find it helpful.

True insight and refined intuition are two concepts intimately related to one another. We can learn "more" from our intuition than from the facts. Often referred to as our "gut feeling" or instinct, it is an incredibly potent force that defies easy explanation. For instance, an individual with extensive experience in the same field is typically more equipped to make intuitive conclusions than someone new to the field. Similarly, some people have a stronger ability to read other people's emotions even when they are not expressed directly. In certain situations, experience and time may improve one's intuition. In others, though, intuition might also be related to unfamiliar or weird individuals or circumstances. Our intuition might not always provide the answers we seek, but it can prompt us to check in further. For instance, you might meet someone for the first time and notice that their "vibes are off." Thus, intuition and insight are related since reaching an insight requires going beyond simplistic explanations of a given circumstance. An insight is anything that, once realized, may appear to be quite clear. In addition, it remains hidden from view unless we are prepared to put in the effort to comprehend something or someone fully. An activated third eye chakra helps us obtain a deeper understanding and sharpens our intuition.

**Enhanced creativity and imagination:** An open third eye chakra inspires us to be more imaginative and self-assured in our creative abilities. You may notice that you're more eager to explore new things. You might even solve difficulties that you have been stuck on for a long time in a creative way. Your third eye is probably more balanced if your perspective changes from fixed to growth-oriented. Furthermore, you can even begin to perceive links between seemingly unrelated things after your awakening.

**Increased self-assurance in being who you are:** It has been observed that living a genuine life is facilitated by an aroused throat chakra. We begin expressing ourselves in a way consistent with our values and identity. However, the throat chakra stage is still a way off from understanding things' actual nature. When the third eye chakra is in balance, we are aware of the environment around us and ourselves. Living authentically in this world is made all the easier by this. We don't feel intimidated by other people's opinions, even while expressing ourselves. We can release our deepest anxieties in numerous ways when our third eye chakra is aligned.

**Decreased tension and anxiety:** Sometimes, the opening of our third eye chakra might result in prophecy (we'll talk more about this in the next chapter), allowing us to look into the future or beyond the material world. This additional information can undoubtedly assist in reducing our worry in both situations. But even if you don't become clairvoyant, the clarity and comprehension that come with this process can greatly lessen stress. In the end, we now know what is important and what isn't and what is worthy of our energy. We are aware of our goals and assets, even in the face of uncertainty. We are less likely to fear the unknown because we can see the big picture of the cosmos.

A stronger feeling of unity with the outside world: Our ability to relate to others is conditioned by our level of self-connection. We may find it difficult to build wholesome relationships with other people if we don't feel confident in who we are. Furthermore, ongoing worry and stress might even cause burnout in us. At this point, it's difficult for us to build deep relationships with other people. Our disconnection can only be exacerbated by feelings of loneliness or misunderstanding. The first thing we do when the third eye chakra is balanced is reconnect with ourselves. Then, as a result of this harmony, everyone who comes into contact with us is impacted. On a deeper level, we may even start to understand that distinctions between us are merely artificial and that we are all the same. We resist the "us versus them" mindset when we regard everyone as heavenly beings. As a result, establishing connections with individuals of diverse origins and opinions becomes considerably simpler.

**Heightened sense of perception:** Our five senses allow us to engage with the outside world. Normally, dealing with significantly too many energies regularly causes these senses to become somewhat muted or overloaded. Our senses restore their strength with the aid of the third eye chakra. You can find yourself appreciating the environment around you more suddenly. Things that you would have otherwise overlooked may come to your attention. As your perceptual talents grow, You might become more aware of environmental changes. This not only gives us access to the planet's wealth but also improves our ability to detect the energy of others.

For instance, highly sensitive persons (HSPs) frequently have the superpower of sensing the energy around them, yet this capacity can occasionally overwhelm HSPs. The secret is to discover our inner harmony.

**An Extremely Optimistic View Of Life:**

Once more, being optimistic in this situation does not mean that we are illusionists about our lives. Our ability to see things positively is facilitated by the clarity we obtain both during and after the awakening experience. First, we learn to accept that sorrow and suffering have a place in this world as we become more open to the world around us. We regard loss, suffering, and sadness as enriching factors rather than as things that take away from the world. Additionally, as waking can deepen our capacity for love, we start to accept the challenges and difficulties in our lives more easily. The benefit of having a balanced third eye chakra may be greatest in maintaining our curiosity. After this, we are excited to explore the world in all its splendor, and days never remain the same. We can, at last, feel like we are in charge of our lives rather than operating on autopilot. But this control is about submitting to the universe's will rather than obstinately controlling every aspect of our lives.

(Hold off for a minute.)

Watch your creative idea now, and let it fade as the orange color returns to its original, sharp state.

(Hold off for ten seconds.)

Bring your mind to another imaginative idea. Experience your thoughts ebb and flow like waves crashing onto a gorgeous beach. Three times over, repeat the visualization.

(Take a two-minute break.)

Return your awareness to your body now. Your sexual and creative energies can flow healthily if you practice clearing and regulating the Swadhisthana chakra.

You will eventually be able to transition between creative pursuits and sexual fantasies with ease. Your need for sex will gradually transform into artistic energy. Your Swadhisthana chakra will be fully balanced at that point.

It is no longer necessary to unblock and balance the Swadhisthana chakra.

With great slowness, move the tips of your fingers. Make gentle movements with your body. Additionally, you are free to adjust your sitting position at any time.

5.

For a minute, keep observing your thoughts.

(Hold off for a minute.)

Now, direct your thoughts to retrieve a particular idea. This idea could relate to something that happened an hour, day, or month ago. Keep your thoughts focused and focused. Remember this particular thought.

(Hold off for ten seconds.)

Now, examine the idea objectively. Permit the idea to fully develop.

(Hold off for ten seconds.)

At this point, focus on your breathing. Your breath enters and exits the vaginal region, which is the location of the Swadhisthana chakra. Your breath has an orange tint. As you breathe in, the orange glow gets brighter and brighter. The orange glow goes away when you exhale.

(Hold off for ten seconds.)

Continue taking short breaths and letting them out. At first, breathing through the Swadhisthana chakra might not be possible. Be at ease. Breathing via the genital area is something you need to practice.

(Hold off for ten seconds.)

The orange glow now encompasses you. Your Swadhisthana chakra is infused with orange.

You're going to see a sexual fantasy now. Assume that the sexual dream is being acted out on the orange glow that covers your genitals. You must pay attention to the genital region and the color orange.

There is a lot of intense sexual imagery. You are having a sexual act on the go. Feel the emotion. Take full advantage of the sexual act. Don't be scared. Don't feel embarrassed.

Just enjoy the graphic sexual content as though it were a motion picture. Examine the graphic. Avoid trying to force your opinions on the sexual notion. Keep out of the way of the visualization. Permit it to occur. Relish the emotion without passing judgment.

(Take a two-minute break.)

Picture your Swadhisthana or sacral chakra. Your genitalia, or the area beneath your navel, is orange in hue. The hue orange appears as a little dot in your mind's eye.

Focus your attention on your ideas.

(Hold off for ten seconds.)

Now, you will carefully and consciously imagine another sexual fantasy. This could be a particular setting or circumstance where you will get sex-related visions. Imagine the dot at your genitalia expanding in size at the same time.

There is a lot of intense sexual imagery. You are having a sexual act on the go. Feel the emotion. Take full advantage of the sexual act. Don't be scared. Don't feel embarrassed.

Just enjoy the graphic sexual content as though it were a motion picture. Examine the graphic. Avoid trying to force your opinions on the sexual notion. Keep out of the way of the visualization. Permit it to occur. Relish the emotion without passing judgment.

If no images come to mind, stay in a condition of non-existence. If you are unable to conjure up a sexual notion, stay obliging. Practitioners who are male or female will have various physical feelings. Don't respond to any physical feelings. Give it up and let it be. Don't hold back any emotions or ideas. Suspend all conclusions and judgments at the same moment.

(Take a two-minute break.)

When people consider having sex, they often feel guilty. Recall that when you are having sex, there is no shame or guilt involved. Your body and mind are entirely focused on the sexual act during those moments of sexual contact. You only feel guilty when you picture sexual imagery.

Consequently, there is a big difference between having sex and engaging in sexual activity. You feel guilty when you fantasize about having sex all the time and without stopping.

As a result, you need to replace ideas that devour sexual energy with creative energies. When your Swadhisthana chakra is balanced, your creative endeavors and sexual urges will coexist.

Now, suddenly and abruptly, let go of the images of sex in your head. Immediately start thinking about something creative. Examine the idea. Writing a sonnet, painting a scene, or completing a pet project are all examples of creative thinking. Allow the orange glow in the background to evoke the concept.

Give the creative process the freedom to go wild. Give the thought room to wander. Watch, but don't respond. Give it a go. Give your creative notion your whole attention.

(Hold off for a minute.)

Now, conjure up another image of a sexual encounter. This is a different scenario and context for this sexual notion. To fully experience this idea, use your imagination. Don't wince or hesitate. Give up. Just keep an eye on the visualization as it unfolds.

Examine the visualization objectively. Avoid getting in the way of your thoughts.

(Take a two-minute break.)

Now, replace the lustful notion with an imaginative one. Three times over, repeat the visualization.

(Take a two-minute break.)

Allow the orange glow to drift toward the psychic horizon, bit by bit. With practice and experience, you'll discover that you can transition between creative thoughts and sensual fantasies with ease. Additionally, your creativity will grow, and you'll start thinking about greater and bigger tasks. You'll start producing more.

Your ideas will come to you naturally. You'll see that another way that sexual energy can be expressed is through creativity. When you can regulate and transform the flow of sexual energy into creative energy, the Swadhisthana chakra will be balanced.

(Take a two-second break.)

A robust sexual urge is necessary. Your body releases happy hormones during sexual activity. These organic fluids are an elixir that encourages a happy and fulfilled existence. Chakra healing specialists never advise giving up on sexual activity completely. The only person who can hope to succeed in life is sexually pleased.

Using Sexual Energy to Drive Manifestation: Developing and Using Sexual Energy

A powerful force with great manifesting power is sexual energy. When deliberately controlled and directed, it can be used as the energy to make our dreams pass. We will look at how to develop and use sexual energy to power your intentions and bring your greatest goals to life in this section.

## Awakening and Directing Sexual Energy via Visualization and Breathwork

Utilizing breathwork and visualization techniques can be an effective way to activate and direct sexual energy. You can increase your ability to produce and channel sexual energy toward your desired manifestations by implementing these strategies into your sexual encounters. Here's how to use visualization and breathwork to awaken and channel sexual energy:

Conscious Inhalation:

Breathe deliberately, slowly, and deeply while you're feeling sexually aroused. Concentrate on bringing your breath to fill your chest, abdomen, and whole body. Envision the breath expanding and circulating into the parts of your body that contain sexual energy.

Visualization of Energy:

Imagine the sexual energy within you as a bright, shining light while you breathe. Observe it growing stronger while you work on your sexual arousal. Allow this energy to enter your body and permeate every cell, saturating your whole being.

Circulation of Energy:

Imagine the sexual energy flowing through certain channels in your body, like the meridian lines or chakras, with every breath. Imagine it flowing in a continuous circle or upward from your base to your crown. The sexual energy in your body is dispersed and amplified by this circulation.

You can expand your ability to harness the transforming potential of sexual energy for manifestation by awakening and channeling it throughout your sexual experiences through the use of breathwork and visualization.

Developing Your Sexual Energy with Both Solo and Coupled Activities

To fully utilize sexual energy's manifestation potential, one must first cultivate it. There are a variety of methods you can experiment with to enhance and develop your sexual energy, regardless of whether you are practicing alone or in a partnership. Here are some actions to think about:

Individual Exercises:

To develop your sexual energy, spend time alone doing activities like self-gratification, meditation, or visualization. You can enhance the intensity of the energy you produce by focusing your intention and attention on developing sexual arousal. Investigate many methods to find the one that speaks to you personally.

Collaborative Methods:

Intimate encounters should be had with a reliable companion to deliberately develop sexual vitality. Using prolonged foreplay, deliberate touch, and mutual breathing exercises, you can establish a space conducive to the development and intensification of sexual energy. To ensure that both partners are on the same page and at ease with the practices, keep the lines of communication open and flowing.

Sacred Sexuality and Tantra:

Examine holy sexuality and the teachings and practices of Tantra. These age-old practices provide fundamental methods for developing sexual energy and fusing it with manifestation and spiritual development. Engaging in techniques like eye gazing, synchronized breathing, and conscious lovemaking can enhance the sexual energy exchanged between partners and strengthen their energetic bond.

You may develop and magnify sexual energy and bring it to the surface for manifestation through both solo and partner practices.

Using Sexual Energy to Energize Thoughts and Bring About Desires

The next step after developing your sexual energy is to channel it toward your goals and aspirations. You can change your intentions with greater strength and hasten the manifestation process by infusing them with the strong sexual energy you have created. Using sexual energy to charge intentions and manifest wishes is how you do this:

With certain intentions:

Ensure your intentions are precise, well-defined, and consistent with your goals. Spend some time outlining your aims in writing, including the precise results you hope to achieve and the accompanying feelings. Your sexual energy will materialize in a concentrated direction if your intentions are clear.

Linkage and Concentration:

Establish a holy area where you can focus your sexual energy and connect with your intentions. Take techniques like visualization or meditation to help you center yourself and focus on the here and now. Focus on the goals you have set for yourself and imagine your life to already be filled with those goals.

Rituals of Sexuality:

Create rituals that integrate the charging of your intentions with sexual energy. This can involve using phrases, symbols, or items to convey your intentions. During sex, intentionally focus your arousal energy on your desires, imagining them to be charged and energized by the strong energy you are creating.

Release of Orgasm:

Concentrate your thoughts and energies on your intentions during the orgasmic moment. Imagine the discharge of sexual energy propelling your intentions into the cosmos with a powerful surge of manifestation energy as you feel it streaming outward. Express your appreciation for the sex energy and the realization of your desires.

You can accelerate the manifestation process by intentionally directing sexual energy into your intentions. Your mind, body, and spirit become in harmony as a result of the increased level of arousal and the release of sexual energy, which generates a strong, concentrated energy that helps you actualize your desires.

Recall that self-awareness, perseverance, and practice are necessary while using sexual energy for manifestation. Respecting your limits, exercising consent, and keeping a healthy, balanced perspective on your sexual experiences are all crucial. By doing this, you may make sure that the development and use of your sexual energy serve your highest benefit and the good of everyone involved.

Within the field of sex magick, the process of developing and using your sexual energy is what propels your desires into reality. You can unlock the immense power of sexual energy as a transformative and manifestation tool by awakening and channeling sexual energy through breathwork and visualization, cultivating sexual energy through solo and partner practices, and using sexual energy to charge intentions and manifest desires.

Accept the sacredness of sexual energy and how it relates to your aspirations. Then, let the fusion of sexual energy and manifestation serve as a calming and enlightening spiritual exercise. You can unite yourself with the creative powers of the universe and invite the manifestation of your deepest dreams and the attainment of your true potential by intentionally working with sexual energy.

Let's use an example of a naturally occurring environmental cycle to better grasp what a chakra is.

In India, the term "TriveniSangam" refers to the confluence of three rivers at a single location. When there is a confluence, the water flows ahead in the center in a circular pattern. As per the teachings of our sages, the human inner body, or 'naadi,' comprises 72,000 thousand entities that facilitate the passage of energy throughout the body.

The word "Nandi" in Hindi refers to extremely tiny blood vessel-like vessels that contain energy.

The energy of self-consciousness runs continuously through the three primary naadi, which are long energy conduits. The Ida, Pingala, and Sushumna are these. The energy flows forward in a cyclical pattern wherever these three naadis converge throughout the body. In spiritual terminology, the gathering point of these energy vessels, or naadi, is called the chakra. Our body exhibits the convergence of these Chakras, also known as naadis, most prominently at seven key locations known as Chakras.

These days, there is a great deal of global discourse on this topic. Numerous scientists are also conducting experiments on this.

In this sense, our life has direction and motion because of the various energy Chakras produce inside our bodies.

We need a distinct kind of energy or power for many bodily functions and aspects of daily life. The center of energy, sometimes called a chakra, is where the greatest amount of energy gathers and circulates within our soul's subtle body or energy body. We will come to see chakras as the form of life values. These life values, or chakras, primarily function from seven distinct locations in our subtle body, which regulate the various bodily systems and organs.

The power of the greatest (strongest) and lowest (weaker) levels of soul consciousness, the effect of its waves, and its completeness are the definitions of chakras given in this book. It will enable you to gain a profound understanding of your existence. Simply put, we are attempting to communicate with you through life values expressed in simple terms by distilling the complex and mystical deep understanding of the energy cycle.

This fantastic book will help the modern generation—or the average man—comprehend their energy levels and may not know much about spirituality.

This book will take you on such a lovely journey that you can comprehend every facet of life. Identifying your shortcomings will be simple. You'll be able to break free from your negative behaviors. Additionally, you won't have any chronic illnesses. Your energy level will be in harmony. You'll overcome your issues, making it possible to quickly achieve the objective of creating a healthy society.

## Which Is The Reason For Energy (Chakra) Imbalance?

Understanding the root cause of Chakra (energy) imbalance can be greatly aided by looking at an example of a sand timer gadget. A sand timer, also known as a sand clock or sand glass, is a tool used to display and measure the passage of time.

A lot of people frequently keep it on their office table. To properly utilize the time while viewing it, one should be conscious of the passing of time.

The sand in this device's upper section keeps slipping downward gradually. The apparatus must be turned upside down so that the sand deposited below will now be up and gently slip down to be dumped below until all of the sand above has fallen into the lower chamber. Within our bodies, energy functions in an identical manner.

When we get up in the morning, we are somewhat balanced with energy, meaning that our entire body is made up of the same quantity of energy from head to toe. There is about equal energy in the top three and bottom three chakras. The center, or heart Chakra, regulates the flow of energy. However, the energy present in the Sahasrara, Ajna, and Vishuddhi Chakras—the three above—gradually decreases as we stand and sit all day. In this instance, our bodies begin to experience two things at once.

First of all, the three Chakras mentioned above store extremely little energy. Second, there is a significant rise in energy inside the lowest three Chakras. As a result, our chakras experience an energy imbalance every day.

The practice of Samadhi is necessary to restore the energy of the unbalanced Chakra. In Sanskrit, Samadhi refers to a condition of carelessness. To reach this state of Samadhi, a great deal of spiritual practice and knowledge are required.

However, God has already bestowed this blessing on all of us—animals and humans. Sleep is that blessing. Indeed, sleep is a simple form of meditation known as Samadhi, during which we effortlessly enter a state of unconsciousness. However, the power gained during this deep slumber, or Samadhi state, is only used the next day.

The spiritual Sanskrit term for this deep sleep is "Sahaj Samadhi." There will be two things that happen even in this simple Samadhi stage.

The first is that we unintentionally join with the cosmic consciousness, from which we temporarily gain universal power; the second is that the body's Chakras all begin to automatically balance. As a result, we gain equilibrium and energy for the next day.

However, this benefit will only be available to those who abide by the laws of nature.

Those who follow their natural path in life enjoy a happy and healthy existence. However, for those who disobey natural principles, refuse to accept life as it unfolds, and quit, life becomes an extremely challenging path.

What is the dharma, or truth, or law of nature? How can I proceed in life's flow? How should I handle it? It will all become clear to you at the end of the book. One can live a healthy and happy life by adhering to these straightforward guidelines.

Throat/Fifth Chakra (Vishuddha)

The thyroid gland and the base of the larynx are where the throat chakra and base of the larynx overlap. In Sanskrit, vishuddha signifies cleansing the body of impurities; body and mind become pure again when this energy point is in harmony. This Chakra is associated with creativity, faith, clear communication, and attentive listening. As a result, the throat chakra is associated with wisdom, planning, communication, and order. The linked organs are the voice cords, ears, throat, and lungs.

Bright blue, the hue linked with this Chakra, is considered peaceful, healing, pure, and comforting. Blue is characterized by space and freedom and is associated with spirituality. Additionally, blue is the color of communication, enabling you to communicate the truth. It symbolizes a pure mind with clarity and optimistic thinking, allowing the body and mind to enjoy tranquility. This Chakra is unbalanced by lies, but it is rebalanced by honesty. Space is associated with the spirit of finding and speaking the truth, both to yourself and those around you, and it can help you become more open to the prospect of expanding your perspective.

An imbalance in this Chakra shows timidity, silence, difficulty thinking properly, and a sense of helplessness. A poor diet, substance misuse, or contaminated air can block this Chakra. There is a communication breakdown when you are out of balance because you cannot listen to yourself or others. It makes you feel alone and misinterpreted. Hormone abnormalities, soreness or stiffness in the neck region, and sore throats are examples of physical symptoms of imbalance.

Creativity, healthy self-expression, purpose fulfillment, and constructive communication are all made possible by a balanced throat Chakra. When you are in balance, you can effectively follow your intuition or your inner self's counsel. You have a thorough and deep understanding of other people.

Singing your favorite songs, taking in the solitude, meditating, chanting affirmations and mantras, eating whole grains and fruits (oranges, apples, etc.), as well as spices (ginger, lemongrass, etc.), and observing the moon reflected on water are the most effective ways to rebalance this Chakra.

### Chakra of the Sixth/Third Eye (Ajna)

The neurological and endocrine systems are connected to the third eye, which is situated in the space between the eyebrows. This Chakra is associated with self-realization, physical development, and intuition. The third eye chakra balances spiritual and physical aspects, promoting equilibrium in the body and mind. It is endowed with the highest knowledge and wisdom. Concentrated third-eye meditation brings about intuitive understanding, emancipation, and the destruction of past-life karma or negative energy.

The sixth Chakra is the hub of intuition, consciousness, perception, and intelligence. The third eye, which connects through inner vision to higher awareness, is thought to provide insights into the future, whereas the two physical eyes are said to observe the past and the present. The Chakra also makes the five senses of the body clearer.

Indigo, the almost black or royal blue color of the third eye chakra, is typically connected to night, whereas light is its element. Indigo is the hue of wisdom and inner knowledge and is thought to open doors to the Divine. In addition to uplifting, the color is thought to assist in transferring energy from the lower chakras into higher spiritual vibrations.

The concept of ultimate wisdom and spiritual enlightenment is strongly supported by the Chakra, also represented by a lotus flower. It is a doorway to greater awareness and directs energy toward universal truth.

If this Chakra is out of balance, it can cause you to feel overly egoistic, timid, or fearful of achievement. Due to its association with the neurological and endocrine systems, this Chakra may present physically as headaches, balance, and vision issues. Neglecting the spiritual or concentrating only on material things can cause unhappiness because it separates you from yourself. Anger, excessive expectations, and the weight and toxicity of the past that obstruct your perspective are common signs of imbalance. Confusion, a lack of direction, melancholy, and indecision are some ways this shows up. Goal-achieving is hampered by self-doubt since it causes a narrow-minded focus. Hallucinations, loneliness, and paranormal experiences are examples of other manifestations.

The third eye chakra necessitates patience and high awareness and is balanced by the freedom of thinking and speech. When your third eye is balanced, it will benefit both your bodily and spiritual wellbeing. This improves feelings, judgment, and inner guidance. Time spent in nature fosters a stronger connection and grounding with the earth while calming overpowering mental impulses. Journaling, channeling, breathwork, yoga (such as headstand poses), meditation in a quiet place, and journaling can all be beneficial. When you're in balance, you feel emotionally, spiritually, and physically balanced, confident, and enthusiastic. You become your own master since you no longer dread death and no longer feel the need to be attached to earthly possessions.

Crown/Seventh Chakra (Sahasrara)

At the top of the head is where the crown chakra is situated. The Sanskrit word for "infinite" or "thousand" is Sahasrara. This Chakra is supposed to be the epicenter of spirituality, enlightenment, and ideas from the highest self. Space is a component of the Chakra and has a close relationship with the brain. This Chakra allows you to access the interior flow of wisdom and universal consciousness. This Chakra is linked to mental abilities like intelligence, memory, and focus. Purple is the equivalent color.

Despite being uncommon, purple is the most potent visible wavelength in the color spectrum. It is considered a spiritual hue that evokes an inner sense of fulfillment, morality, spirituality, curiosity, and increased self-awareness. It helps you focus and practice introspection and has a relaxing yet energetic effect on the body.

Such as boredom, despair, and frustration surface. Inflexibility in thought, blindness to opposing viewpoints, resistance to learning new information, worldly attachment, and a lack of connection or grounding are further examples. Parkinson's disease, depression, issues with coordination, and a variety of mental diseases are examples of related disorders.

Energy from all the other chakras flows into the crown chakra, so balancing and healing this Chakra requires addressing the other six first. This Chakra is balanced by all whole meals, violet foods (such as eggplant, red/black grapes, etc.), ginger spice, and herbal teas. Yoga, meditation, and spending time in nature are also advised. A balanced chakra results in a positive outlook on life, expressed through positive adjustments to your behaviors and attitudes. Your inner direction, rather than the ego, comes from a place of gratitude, compassion, and acceptance of yourself and others. You avoid stress-inducing and unhappy circumstances, feelings, and ideas, but you also avoid being hooked to happy emotions that are in balance. Greater spiritual insight, harmony, tranquility, and perspective clarity are experienced when things are balanced. The full balance of this Chakra signifies completion.

Organizing and Purifying:

It's important to clear and purify your energy field before diving into chakra healing. Stuck or negative energy might make healing more difficult. A purifying bath or shower, smudging with sage or palosanto, or envisioning a waterfall of cleansing light flowing over your body are just a few ways to clear and cleanse your energy. Decide to let go of any unwelcome energy or feelings that might obstruct your chakras so that healing and transformation can occur.

Wellbeing and Self-Care:

Make your wellbeing and self-care a priority while preparing for chakra healing. Take part in good things for your health, mind, and soul. Maintain hydration, exercise frequently, get enough restful sleep, and eat a balanced, healthful diet. Include techniques like yoga, meditation, and journaling that help people unwind and reduce stress. Chakra healing can be strengthened and your general wellbeing supported when you take comprehensive care of yourself.

Transparency and Giving Up:

Have an open mind and heart as you embark on your chakra healing adventure. Develop an inquisitive, open-mindedness and eagerness to discover your inner self. Let go of whatever expectations or ideas you may have about how your healing process will turn out. Give yourself over to the process, believing it will work out for your best and highest good. Accept the uncertainty and be receptive to the revelations, healing, and metamorphosis that come with chakra healing.

Seek Advice and Assistance:

Seek assistance from seasoned practitioners or teachers if you are new to chakra healing or need more direction. They can offer insightful advice, practical methods, and tailored direction to improve your chakra healing process. Attend seminars, workshops, or one-on-one consultations to improve your knowledge and skills.

A vital first step in maximizing the efficacy of your chakra healing journey is preparation. You lay a solid foundation for profound healing and change by educating yourself, setting intentions, making a sacred place, grounding, centering, clearing, and purifying, putting self-care first, accepting openness and surrender, and asking for help and support.

The advantages of your chakra healing practice will be amplified if you take the time to prepare yourself mentally, physically, and emotionally. When approaching your chakra healing path with clarity, intention, and openness, you make yourself more vulnerable to deep healing and personal development.

In the upcoming chapters, we shall explore certain methods and practices for chakra healing. By incorporating the preparation procedures covered in this chapter, you will be prepared to embark on a life-changing path of self-healing, personal development, and chakra healing.

Space for Meditation or an Altar:

Set up an altar or meditation place to provide a focal point in your sacred space. This allotted area represents your spirituality and personal development tangibly. The following are some components you could use:

**Altar Cloth:** To place on the altar, pick a cloth that expresses your spirituality or sense of style.

Light candles to represent the presence of heavenly energy and to create a serene, hallowed atmosphere.

Use basic white candles or colorful candles that correlate to each Chakra.

During your chakra healing exercise, you can improve the sensory experience and purify the area using essential oils or burning incense.

**Sacred artifacts:** Arrange important trinkets, statues or figurines of deities, or artifacts of personal value on the altar.

Sacred Customs & Traditions:

Take part in sacred practices and rituals in your sacred area to strengthen your energy and connection. Here are some recommendations:

Set aside time for meditation to help you center yourself, calm your thoughts, and establish a connection with your inner self.

**Prayer:** Express your thanks, intentions, and prayers to the higher force or deity that speaks to you.

**Journaling:** Write down your ideas and experiences in a journal or use your sacred space for introspection and self-expression.

**Ceremonies & Rituals:** Construct heartfelt ceremonies or rituals that support your spiritual values and wellbeing goals. For instance, you may do a full moon ceremony or carry out a chakra balancing ritual.

**Deep Diving Heart Chakra Reflections**

It is common knowledge that choosing to comprehend—selecting forgiveness and compassion over condemnation and resentment—is the key to opening up to receiving and giving unconditional love and connecting with and balancing your Heart chakra.

When we discuss selecting compassion over judgment, we mean letting go of self-criticism and judgment and selecting self-acceptance, self-love, and self-compassion instead. One of the most effective ways to open your Heart chakra is to decide to love and care for yourself.

Identifying certain problems in our behavior and breaking through ingrained emotional patterns might be challenging. The next step is deep reflection, which comes after you have evaluated the condition of your own Heart Center and gained an understanding of the Heart Chakra and its function in your mind and body. Guided reflection is the most effective method for exposing your deeply held beliefs and ideas to truly and permanently heal the heart chakra.

The ideas and people that come to mind for you and make you feel bad are messengers for you as you consider the journal exercises and questions below.

They serve as messengers for the aspects of you that are still wounded. Learning to follow our wounds' guidance is the key to the chakra healing process. While considering the questions and/or suggestions in this chapter, remember to treat yourself with kindness and compassion. Answer with total honesty and compassion, letting go of self-judgment and self-criticism, and reflect with an open heart and mind.

The following questions and prompts are intended to open, activate, and support the healing of your heart chakra. Don't forget to block out time each day for at least the next week in your planner or calendar to consider the following questions. You might feel reluctant or resistant to going deeply into self-reflection because uncomfortable emotions might surface. However, this is precisely where journaling and introspection become powerful. It presents an opportunity to work with our subconscious minds and the dark side of our souls, also known as the "shadow" side.

Recall that you are not obligated to record everything in writing if you choose. Just be sure you are taking your time to look for sincere, truthful responses to every query and record any insights or epiphanies you have. Journaling may stay superficial if you don't take the effort to delve deeper and reveal the layers of your feelings, ideas, and beliefs. Give yourself the process of letting go of your feelings and ideas. Take your time and ensure you are in an area without interruptions or distractions.

Heart Chakra Meditations

Can I have empathy for both myself and other people?

Do I give and accept love from myself?

Is it possible for me to love without conditions?

Is there someone or something I need to forgive and let go of because I'm holding it in my heart?

Can I let go of past hurts? For my heart to open and heal, can I find a deeper level of acceptance and forgiveness for myself and others?

Can I accept others for who they are and myself for who I am?

Do I deserve to be loved? Can I earn my love?

How can I show the people in my life that I love them? Can I show love to other people with ease? How can I show myself love? Can I show myself love without much difficulty?

Do I have emotional problems that prevent me from loving or feeling loved, making my heart closed?

Do I feel appreciative of all my blessings?

Is it okay for me to "feel for" and empathize with others?

Do I sense my relationship with others?

Do I feel at ease giving? Who am I "giving" to?"

What does love that isn't conditional mean to me?

What aspects of my surroundings make me feel like I'm a part of them, and what aspects make me feel alone? How do I foster that sense of belonging?

Is my tendency to trust people natural? Can I put too much trust in people or withhold my trust?

Which three times in my life did I feel incredibly loved? Describe your feelings at these times.

1.3 The Mantras' Philosophical Foundation

Mantra theory is deeply ingrained in Indian subcontinental spiritual and intellectual traditions, particularly in Eastern spiritual approaches like Buddhism and Hinduism. Mantras communicate the essence of cosmic truths and reflect profound philosophical ideas. To comprehend the meaning behind mantras, one must know their significance, resonance, and role in the spiritual path.

1. Sacred Sound and Vibration: Sound is viewed as an essential component of creation and the universe in the mantra philosophy. The ancient sages and seers saw the universe as a manifestation of sound waves. They held that the sacred sound of "Om" or "AUM," often called the

primordial sound or the cosmic song of creation, created the universe. Mantras are thought to be powerful, concentrated sounds that carry particular vibrations and energies.

2. The Power of Resonance: When mantras are chanted or recited continuously, both the practitioner and the surroundings resonate. The purpose of this resonance is to align the practitioner's chakras, or energy centers, with the vibrations of the cosmos. Achieving harmony between human and global energies facilitates spiritual transformation and elevates consciousness.

3. Invocation of the Divine: Mantras are associated with specific gods or

cosmic energies. The goal of practitioners' mantras is to invoke the blessings and favor of these deities or forces. Mantra chanting creates a strong bond between the devotee and the divine and fosters devotion.

4. Power of Focus and Purpose: Mantras' effectiveness depends critically on the intention behind their recitation. Mantras can be focused and sincerely repeated to help clear the mind, reduce mental noise, and encourage inner focus. The mind becomes more receptive to spiritual revelations and higher truths as it becomes more focused.

5. Metamorphosis and Introspection:

Mantras are considered transforming tools that have the power to purify and elevate the practitioner's awareness. When a person learns their true essence beyond the limitations of their ego, regular and consistent mantra practice may result in self-realization. A deeper understanding of how everything is interconnected results from this awareness.

6. Energy Impact: It is believed that mantras affect the practitioner's mental state and immediate surroundings. Mantras' uplifting and serene vibrations have the potential to cleanse and purify the environment.

7. Language and Sacredness: Mantras are typically formed in Sanskrit and other ancient languages, revered for their precise and powerful phonetic

patterns. The Sanskrit language is believed to possess a special spiritual force and is innately connected to the divine.

8. Mantras as Spiritual Progress Instruments: These sacred sounds are viewed as helpful instruments for self-discovery and spiritual advancement in the mantra concept. Practitioners use mantras to break free from the limitations of the material world, ascend to higher states of consciousness, and ultimately achieve spiritual liberation (moksha).

Mantras are based, in essence, on the understanding that sound is a powerful force in the universe and the belief that repeating sacred sounds can result in profound spiritual growth. Using mantras can help you reach higher states of consciousness, purify your mind, and call upon the divine on your path to spiritual liberation and self-realization.

The Energy Healing System and Chakra System

An alternative form of treatment called energy healing uses the body's energy system to aid mental, spiritual, and physical recovery. Balance the chakras; energy healers employ a variety of techniques.

Some people get amazing results when using various forms of energy healing to help them overcome various ailments they face. Although there hasn't been much scientific research in this area yet, one study concluded that energy healing helps people relax and reduce stress (Anderson, Wisneski, 2005).

Reiki

Reiki is a popular energy healing method in which the hands of the practitioner are used to channel energy into the body. The practitioner places their hands on or close to the chakras to balance and activate them and support healing and wellbeing.

Crystal Therapy

You can use crystals to support your physical, emotional, and spiritual wellbeing—they're not just pretty stones! Using the distinct energy signatures of various crystals, crystal healing is a technique that can help balance your chakras and improve your general health.

Every crystal has unique qualities that can be applied to enhance various facets of your wellbeing wellbeing. For instance, balance your crown chakra with amethyst to increase your spiritual awareness. Feelings of love and compassion if you need emotional healing. Putting crystals in the precise spots on your body that correspond to each chakra is a common way to use them. Additionally, you could wear them as jewelry or carry them around all day. A crystal can assist with boosting self-confidence, shielding against bad energy, or feeling more rooted and balanced.

What's the best part, then? Other energy work techniques, such as Reiki and meditation, produce life-changing results.

Vibrant Healing

A fascinating "sound healing" therapy uses sound waves to enhance general well-being. It focuses on the chakras, our body's seven energy centers that affect our mental, emotional, and spiritual aspects. Tuning forks and the human voice are used by sound healing practitioners to produce strong vibrations that resonate with each chakra, fostering harmony and balance.

Imagine yourself lying down and feeling the sound waves of a singing bowl pulsing through your body, enveloping you in a wave of calm and peace. Or maybe you're experiencing profound relaxation and inner serenity while participating in a group sound healing session while the deep vibrations of gongs and tuning forks fill the room. A handful of the experiences that sound healing can provide are listed here.

For centuries, various cultures have employed sound healing for both spiritual and physical healing. It is increasingly acknowledged as a useful tool for encouraging balance and wellbeing in our hectic and frequently stressful lives.

It is crucial to remember that the data presented here is meant solely for general informational purposes and should not be used in place of expert medical advice, diagnosis, or treatment. You must know if you are having serious health issues. Avoiding or postponing medical care can have detrimental effects that could endanger life. You should always speak with a medical professional if you have any questions or concerns about your health. The information on this platform is not meant to replace your healthcare provider's advice or recommendations.

In the book series, we will delve deeper into energy healing and its connection to the Chakras, so please stay tuned.

Chapter 1: Crown Chakra

The human mind yearns for unity, awareness, and knowledge to fulfill all other needs. Each person's quest for knowledge takes on a different topic based on their interests and personality; some study spirituality in great detail, while others adopt a more academic or practical approach. Despite these differences, the fundamentals of knowledge are always the same. One of the humans' most intense needs is a sense of oneness. When we see how everything is interconnected in a complex, elaborate tapestry, where each thread contributes to the others and has a vital role, we experience a sense of enlightenment.

The crown, also known as the Sahasrara chakra, is located at the top of the chakra hierarchy and the top of the head (Olesen, 2014). We are connected to spiritual divinity and the universe through this chakra. The concept that everything in the universe is interconnected and that we are all the same underpins this chakra. Enlightenment, awareness, and freedom from most judgmental tendencies are associated with an open crown chakra.

An underactive crown causes obstinate, unyielding thinking, a refusal to accept opposing viewpoints, and a determination that your beliefs are true regardless of the evidence against them. An overactive crown chakra indicates that you are overanalyzing situations and becoming so preoccupied with mental or spiritual matters that you neglect your other needs, physical well-being, or social life.

When an individual experiences excessive attachment, the crown chakra may become off-balanced. This bond can be formed with a location, material possessions, a concept or way of thinking, or an individual. The individual grows increasingly reliant on the object of their attachment and finds it impossible to imagine life without it. Generally speaking, they have tunnel vision and cannot perceive the situation rationally. The person feels that they have no right to know anything that contradicts their limited perspective, and this imbalance violates that right.

Sensitivity to light and sound, neurological conditions, conceit, entitlement, restlessness, boredom, sleep disorders, mental illnesses, learning disabilities, and even comas have all been linked to closed or imbalanced crown chakras.

Silence feeds the crown chakra, just as it did the third eye chakra before it. To open the crown chakra, turn off background noise whenever you can and make mental space. Fortunately, when you find yourself at this last chakra in the system, you've probably had a lot of experience grounding yourself, clearing your mind, and achieving a calm state.

For the ultimate crown chakra, you can use all the techniques you've used to open and support the other chakras. The crown chakra can benefit from a variety of practices, including journaling, spending time in nature, paying attention to your body and self, meditation, using essential oils and incense, chanting mantras and positive affirmations like "Ohm" or "I am divine," and engaging in creative endeavors that balance the lower chakras.

This one is the most universal of the seven chakras since it doesn't correlate with any particular diet or set of practices. Since the main components of this chakra are light and thoughtfulness, it is beneficial to engage in logical activities and pay particular attention to learning and thoughtfulness. This could involve reading, studying various materials, solving puzzles, and playing strategy or logic-based games. Getting plenty of soft natural light in your surroundings can also help heal the crown chakra. Consider adjusting the lighting to make your home and workspace as comfortable as possible.

Foods and Beverages

Pure foods are what you'll need to clear the seventh chakra. Choose produce that has been grown organically whenever possible. A salad with leafy vegetables and homemade dressing is one of the best foods to support your crown chakra. Additionally, prepare your food in clear glass dinnerware. Fasting and detoxifying at least once a year also helps.

Related Crystals

Moonstone, Sugilite, Labradorite, and Amethyst

The aura is cleansed by amethyst. It is among the most spiritual of stones with a high spiritual vibration. It strengthens psychic abilities, spiritual awareness, wisdom, and intuition. It is a naturally occurring tranquilizer that calms the mind and emotions. For this reason, it works well in treating insomnia. It calms agitation, fear, anger, and anxiety. It facilitates the removal of obstacles and addictions (of all kinds). It improves a higher state of consciousness and meditation. It improves visualization and aids in dream interpretation. It opens the throat and uppermost chakras. However, paranoia and schizophrenia should not be treated with this crystal.

www.ingramcontent.com/pod-product-compliance
Lightning Source LLC
Chambersburg PA
CBHW052138110526
44591CB00012B/1770